GIN

CLASSIC &
CONTEMPORARY
COCKTAILS

An Hachette UK Company
www.hachette.co.uk

First published in Great Britain in 2018 by Hamlyn,
an imprint of Octopus Publishing Group Ltd
Carmelite House, 50 Victoria Embankment, London EC4Y 0DZ
www.octopusbooks.co.uk

Distributed in the US by
Hachette Book Group
1290 Avenue of the Americas
4th and 5th Floors
New York, NY 10104

Distributed in Canada by
Canadian Manda Group
664 Annette St.
Toronto, Ontario, Canada M6S 2C8

ISBN 978-0-75373-310-3

A CIP catalogue record for this book is available from the British Library

Printed and bound in China

10 9 8 7 6 5

Publisher: Lucy Pessell
Designer: Lisa Layton
Editor: Sarah Vaughan
Production Controller: Dasha Miller
Cover and interior motifs created by: Abhimanyu Bose, LSE Designs, Magicon, Valeriy,
Wuppdidu. All from *The Noun Project*.

The measure that has been used in the recipes is based on a bar jigger, which is 25 ml (1 fl oz).
If preferred, a different volume can be used, providing the proportions are kept constant within a
drink and suitable adjustments are made to spoon measurements, where they occur.

Standard level spoon measurements are used in all recipes.
1 tablespoon = one 15 ml spoon
1 teaspoon = one 5 ml spoon

This book contains cocktails made with raw or lightly cooked eggs. It is prudent for more vulnerable
people to avoid uncooked or lightly cooked cocktails made with eggs.

Some of this material previously appeared in *Hamlyn All Colour Cookery: 200 Classic Cocktails* and
501 Must-Drink Cocktails.

GIN

CLASSIC &
CONTEMPORARY
COCKTAILS

hamlyn

CONTENTS

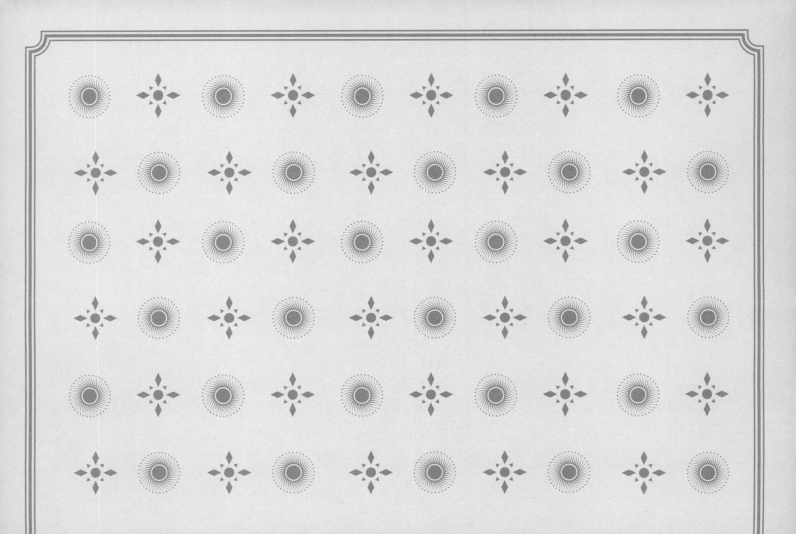

A BRIEF HISTORY OF GIN & COCKTAILS

The origin of the word 'COCKTAIL' is widely disputed.

Initially used to describe the docked tails of horses that were not thoroughbred (which hasn't much to do with a Singapore Sling), the alleged first definition of a 'cocktail' appeared in New York's *The Balance and Columbian Repository*. In response to the question 'What is a cocktail?' the editor replied: 'it is a stimulating liquor, composed of spirits of any kind, sugar, water and bitters... in as much as it renders the heart stout and bold, at the same time that it fuddles the head... because a person, having swallowed a glass of it, is ready to swallow anything else.' Which sounds a little more like it.

However it began, this delightful act of mixing varying amounts of spirits, sugar and bitters has evolved, after decades of fine crafting, experimentation and even 13 years of prohibition in the United States, into the 'cocktail' we know and love. Each one a masterpiece. Each one to be made just right for you.

In the century since Harry Craddock concocted the Corpse Reviver and the White Lady, James Bond has insisted on breaking the number 1 rule to not shake a Martini every time he goes to the bar, and *Sex and the City* has introduced a whole new generation of drinkers to the very pink, very fabulous, Cosmopolitan cocktail. And the idea it can be paired with a burger and fries. Which is fine by us.

Go forth and make yours a Martini. Or a French Afternoon at gin o'clock on a mizzly Monday morning.

GIN is (usually) a clear spirit distilled from grain or malt and then flavoured with juniper berries and other botanical products.

The name Gin is derived from the French *genièvre,* or the Dutch *jenever* – both meaning 'juniper' (and both harder to pronounce than the Latin 'juniperus').

Hailing from early 17th century Holland, Gin was initially produced as a medicine rather than a spirit, to which juniper was added only to make it more palatable. Thank you, Medicine.

Gin has come a long way since then. Once given to soothe stomach complaints and warm troops at war, it has established itself as one of the most popular spirits and is known to alleviate the downs (and boost the ups) of the head and heart, and warm troops at the bar.

It's at the heart of celebrated classic cocktails such as the Martini, Singapore Sling, Negroni and Tom Collins (the list is, thankfully, endless), and this oh–so versatile spirit deserves the role of 'truly magic ingredient number one' in a host of modern twists and contemporary concoctions.

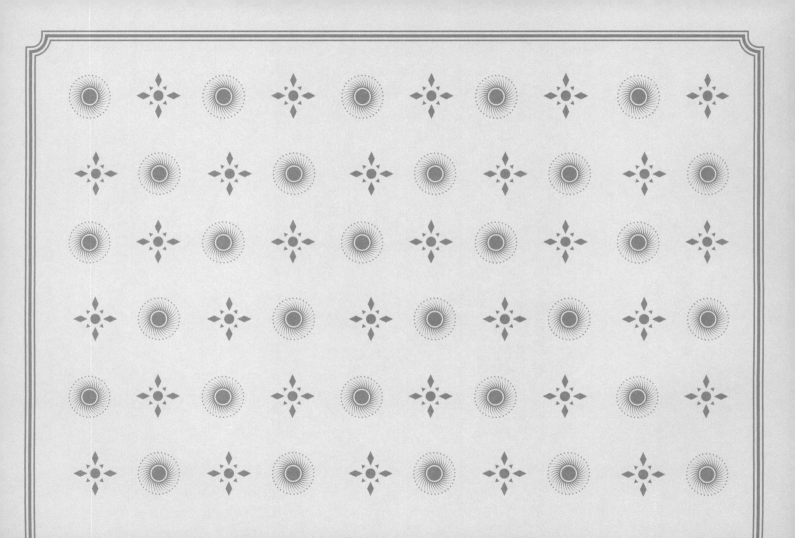

LIGHT & FLORAL

GIN CUCUMBER COOLER

2 MEASURES GIN

5 MINT LEAVES

5 SLICES CUCUMBER

3 MEASURES APPLE JUICE

3 MEASURES SODA WATER

MINT, TO GARNISH

Add the gin, mint and cucumber to a glass and gently muddle.

Leave to stand for a couple of minutes, then add the apple juice, soda water and some ice cubes.

Garnish with a sprig of mint.

EDEN'S CLUB COLLINS

2 MEASURES CUCUMBER-INFUSED GIN

(SEE PAGE 115)

2 TSP ELDERFLOWER LIQUEUR

2 TSP LEMON JUICE

2 MEASURES APPLE JUICE

5 MINT LEAVES

SODA WATER, TO TOP

APPLE OR MINT, TO GARNISH

Add all the ingredients except the soda water to a cocktail shaker and shake and strain into an ice-filled sling glass.

Top up with soda water and garnish with an apple slice or mint sprig.

ORCHARD COLLINS

1 MEASURE GIN

3 TSP LEMON JUICE

3 TSP CAMOMILE & FENNEL SEED SHRUB

1 MEASURE APPLE JUICE

CIDER, TO TOP

APPLE, TO GARNISH

Add all the ingredients except the cider to a cocktail shaker and shake and strain into a collins glass filled with ice cubes.

Top up with 4 measures cider and garnish with an apple slice.

15

CAMOMILE COLLINS

2 MEASURES GIN

1 CAMOMILE TEA BAG

1 MEASURE LEMON JUICE

1 MEASURE SUGAR SYRUP

4 MEASURES SODA WATER

LEMON, TO GARNISH

Pour the gin into a glass and add the tea bag.

Stir the tea bag and gin together, for about 5 minutes, until the gin is infused with camomile flavour.

Remove the tea bag and fill the glass with ice cubes.

Add the remaining ingredients and garnish with a lemon slice.

FRENCH AFTERNOON

1 MEASURE GIN

3 TSP CAMOMILE TEA SYRUP

3 TSP LEMON JUICE

2 DASHES PEACH BITTERS

CHAMPAGNE, TO TOP

LEMON, TO GARNISH

Add all the ingredients except the Champagne to a cocktail shaker and shake and strain into a flute glass.

Top up with 4 measures chilled Champagne and garnish with a lemon twist.

CITRUS HIGHBALL

1 MEASURE GIN

1 CITRUS TEA BAG

LOW-CALORIE TONIC WATER, TO TOP

LIME OR ORANGE, TO GARNISH

Place the gin and citrus tea bag in a collins glass and leave to infuse for 2 minutes.

Remove the tea bag, fill the glass with ice cubes and top up with 4 measures low-calorie tonic water.

Stir, then garnish with a lime or orange wedge.

GIN GARDEN MARTINI

4 MEASURES GIN

1 MEASURE ELDERFLOWER CORDIAL

½ CUCUMBER, PEELED & CHOPPED

2 MEASURES PRESSED APPLE JUICE

CUCUMBER, TO GARNISH

Muddle the cucumber in the bottom of a cocktail shaker with the elderflower cordial.

Add the gin, apple juice and some ice cubes and shake and double-strain into 2 chilled martini glasses.

Garnish with peeled cucumber slices.

GIN & TONIC

2 MEASURES GIN

4 MEASURES TONIC WATER

LIME, TO GARNISH

Pour the gin into a highball glass filled with cubed ice.

Top with tonic water and garnish with a lime wedge.

HONG KONG SLING

½ MEASURE GIN

½ MEASURE LYCHEE LIQUEUR

1 MEASURE LYCHEE PURÉE

1 MEASURE LEMON JUICE

½ MEASURE SUGAR SYRUP

SODA WATER, TO TOP

FRESH LYCHEE IN ITS SHELL, TO GARNISH

Add all the ingredients except the soda water to a cocktail shaker and shake and strain into a sling glass.

Top up with soda water, garnish with a lychee and serve with long straws.

ABBEY ROAD

2 MEASURES GIN

½ MEASURE LEMON JUICE

1 MEASURE APPLE JUICE

6 MINT LEAVES

1 PIECE CANDIED GINGER

LEMON & MINT, TO GARNISH

Muddle the mint leaves, ginger and lemon juice in a cocktail shaker and then add all the remaining ingredients and shake well.

Strain into an old-fashioned glass over crushed ice and garnish with a lemon wedge and a mint sprig.

STRAWBERRY FIELDS

2 MEASURES GIN

1 CAMOMILE TEA BAG

1 MEASURE STRAWBERRY PURÉE

2 TSP LEMON JUICE

1 MEASURE DOUBLE CREAM

3 TSP EGG WHITE

SODA WATER, TO TOP

STRAWBERRY, TO GARNISH

Place 1 camomile tea bag and 2 measures gin in a cocktail shaker and leave to infuse for 2 minutes.

Remove the tea bag and add the rest of the ingredients to the shaker.

Shake and strain into a wine glass and top up with 4 measures chilled soda water.

Garnish with a strawberry.

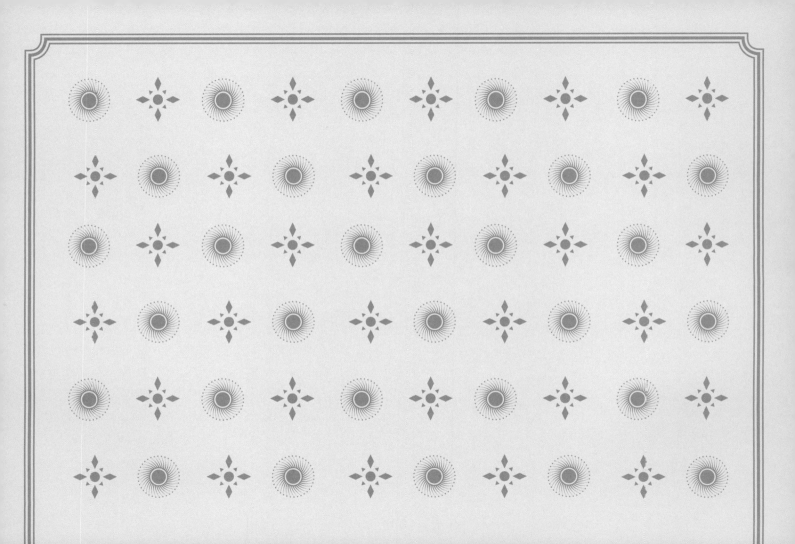

GINNY GIN FIZZ

2 MEASURES GIN

1 CAMOMILE TEA BAG

1 MEASURE LEMON JUICE

1 MEASURE SUGAR SYRUP

3 TSP EGG WHITE

SODA WATER, TO TOP

LEMON, TO GARNISH

Place the tea bag and gin in a cocktail shaker and leave to infuse for 2 minutes.

Remove the tea bag, add the rest of the ingredients and shake and strain into a wine glass filled with ice cubes.

Top up with the soda water and garnish with a lemon twist.

ROYAL COBBLER

1 MEASURE GIN

½ MEASURE RASPBERRY SYRUP

½ MEASURE LEMON JUICE

1 MEASURE PINEAPPLE JUICE

PROSECCO, TO TOP

RASPBERRIES, TO GARNISH

Add all the ingredients except the Prosecco to a cocktail shaker and shake well.

Strain into a rocks glass filled with cubed ice and top with Prosecco.

Garnish with raspberries.

SUNSHINE STATE

1 MEASURE GIN

½ MEASURE ELDERFLOWER LIQUEUR

2 TSP LEMON JUICE

1 MEASURE APPLE JUICE

6 MINT LEAVES

PROSECCO, TO TOP

STRAWBERRY, TO GARNISH

Squeeze the mint leaves in your hand to express the oils, then drop them into a highball glass.

Add the gin, elderflower liqueur, lemon juice and apple juice, fill with cubed ice and top with chilled Prosecco.

Stir briefly and garnish with slices of strawberry.

31

SWEET SIXTEEN

2 MEASURES GIN

JUICE OF ½ LIME

2 DASHES GRENADINE

1 TSP SUGAR SYRUP

BITTER LEMON, TO TOP

LEMON, TO GARNISH

Add some ice cubes and all the ingredients, except the bitter lemon, to a cocktail shaker and shake well until a frost forms.

Fill a highball glass with ice cubes, strain the cocktail over it and top up with bitter lemon.

Garnish with a lemon rind strip.

NEHRU

1 MEASURE GIN

4 SLICES MANGO

5 PINK PEPPERCORNS

PROSECCO, TO TOP

Add the gin, mango and peppercorns to a blender or food processor and blend until smooth.

Strain into a Champagne flute and top with chilled Prosecco.

33

SOUTHSIDE

2 MEASURES GIN

4 TSP LIME JUICE

4 TSP SUGAR SYRUP

5 MINT LEAVES

MINT, TO GARNISH

Add all the ingredients to a cocktail shaker and shake and strain into a cocktail glass.

Garnish with a mint leaf.

FAIR LADY

1 MEASURE GIN

1 DASH COINTREAU

4 MEASURES GRAPEFRUIT JUICE

LIGHTLY BEATEN EGG WHITE

CASTER SUGAR

Frost the rim of an old-fashioned glass by dipping it into egg white and pressing it into the sugar.

Add the remaining ingredients, including the egg white and some ice cubes, into a cocktail shaker.

Shake well, then pour into the prepared glass.

TIPPERARY

3 MEASURES GIN

3 MEASURES DRY VERMOUTH

JUICE OF 1 LEMON

Add all the ingredients, including some ice cubes, into a mixing glass.

Stir gently and strain into a chilled cocktail glass.

MARTINEZ

2 MEASURES GIN

3 TSP SWEET VERMOUTH

2 TSP ORANGE LIQUEUR

2 DASHES ANGOSTURA BITTERS

ORANGE, TO GARNISH

Fill a glass with ice and add the remaining ingredients.

Stir and garnish with an orange twist.

SLOE-HO

2 MEASURES SLOE GIN

1 MEASURE LEMON JUICE

½ MEASURE SUGAR SYRUP

½ MEASURE EGG WHITE

SODA WATER, TO TOP

LEMON, TO GARNISH

Add all the ingredients except the soda water into a cocktail shaker and shake well.

Strain into a highball glass filled with ice cubes and top up with soda water.

Garnish with a long lemon rind spiral.

HONEY DEW

1 MEASURE GIN

½ MEASURE LEMON JUICE

½ MEASURE SUGAR SYRUP

2 DROPS ABSINTHE (OR PERNOD)

5 CUBES HONEYDEW MELON

PROSECCO, TO TOP

LEMON & ROSEMARY, TO GARNISH

Add all the ingredients except the Prosecco to a blender or food processor and blend with 5 cubes of ice.

Pour into a chilled wine glass, top with chilled Prosecco and garnish with a lemon twist and a sprig of rosemary.

41

KIWI
SMASH

2 MEASURES GIN

½ KIWI FRUIT, QUARTERED

4 SLICES LEMON

4 TSP SUGAR SYRUP

1 SPRIG CORIANDER

KIWI FRUIT, TO GARNISH

Add the kiwi fruit, lemon and sugar syrup to a glass and muddle.

Add the gin and coriander and half-fill the glass with crushed ice.

Churn with the muddler until thoroughly mixed and top up with more crushed ice.

Garnish with a kiwi fruit slice.

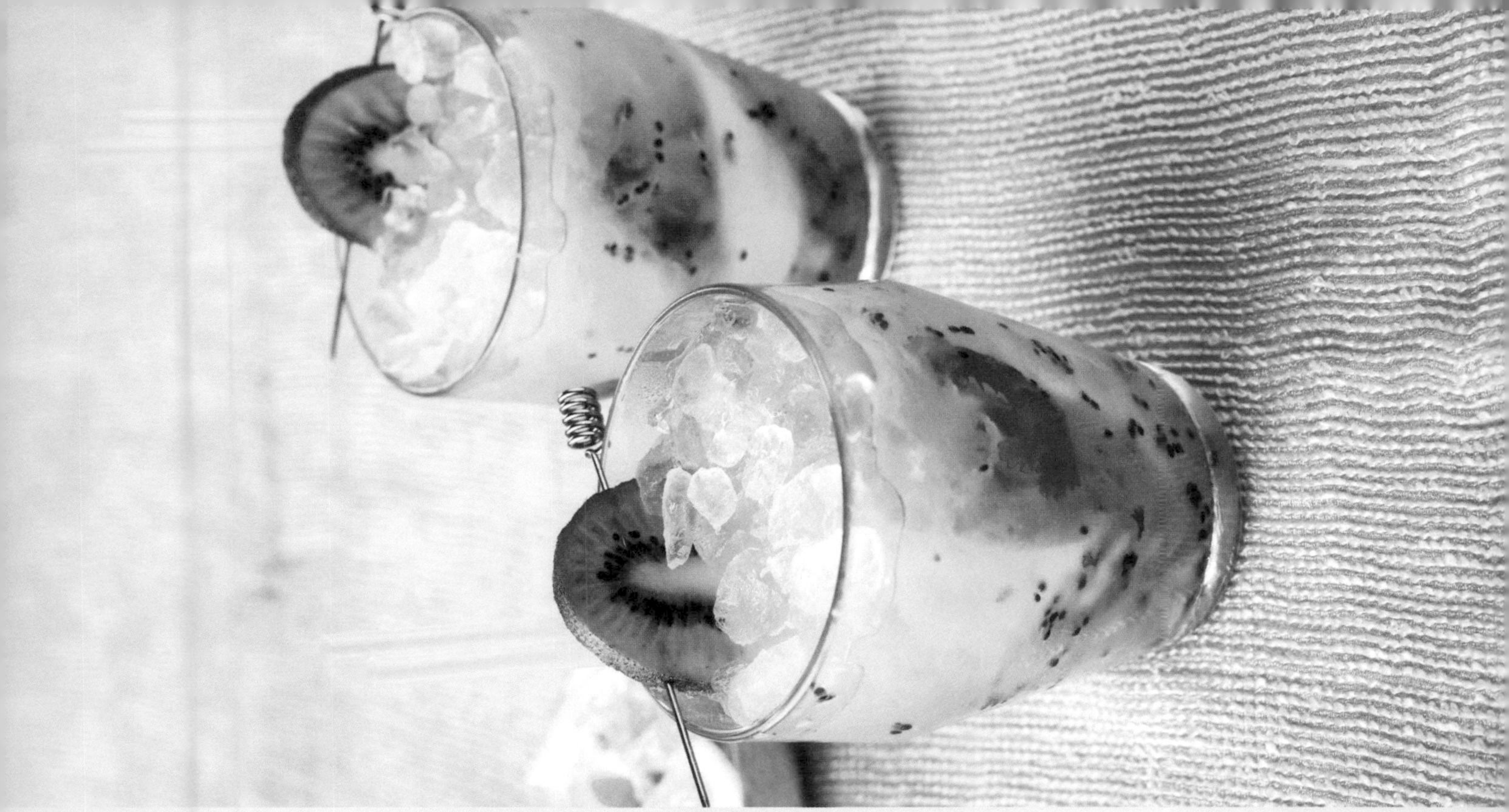

GINTY COLLINS

2 MEASURES GIN

1 EARL GREY TEA BAG

2 TSP GRAPEFRUIT LIQUEUR

1 MEASURE LEMON JUICE

1 MEASURE SUGAR SYRUP

GRAPEFRUIT BITTERS

GRAPEFRUIT, TO GARNISH

Pour 2 measures gin into a collins glass and add 1 Earl Grey tea bag. Allow to infuse for 1 minute before removing the tea bag.

Fill the glass with ice cubes and add the rest of the ingredients and stir gently.

Garnish with a grapefruit twist.

SMOKEY MARTINI

4 MEASURES GIN

2 MEASURES SLOE GIN

½ MEASURE DRY VERMOUTH

10 DROPS ORANGE BITTERS

ORANGE, TO GARNISH

Put some ice cubes into a mixing glass, add ½ measure dry vermouth and stir until the ice cubes are well coated.

Pour in the gin and sloe gin then add 10 drops orange bitters.

Stir well, strain into 2 chilled cocktail glasses and garnish with an orange twist.

BETSY

2 MEASURES GIN OR VODKA

4 TSP LIME JUICE

1 MEASURE SUGAR SYRUP

2 STRAWBERRIES

1 SPRIG CORIANDER

STRAWBERRIES, TO GARNISH

Add all the ingredients, plus a cup of ice cubes, to a food processor or blender and blend until smooth.

Pour into 2 glasses and garnish each with a strawberry.

47

THE FIX

4 MEASURES GIN

1 MEASURE COINTREAU

1 DASH LIME JUICE

1 DASH LEMON JUICE

1 DASH PINEAPPLE JUICE

Add all the ingredients to a cocktail shaker filled with ice.

Shake and strain into 2 chilled highball glasses.

GREEN BAY COLADA

2 MEASURES GIN

1 TSP GINGER JUICE

2 TSP LEMON JUICE

1 MEASURE AGAVE SYRUP

½ KIWI FRUIT, PEELED

5 CUBES CANTALOUPE MELON

1 SPRIG CORIANDER

KIWI FRUIT, TO GARNISH

Add all the ingredients and 1 cup ice cubes to a food processor or blender and blend until smooth.

Pour into a sling glass and garnish with a kiwi slice.

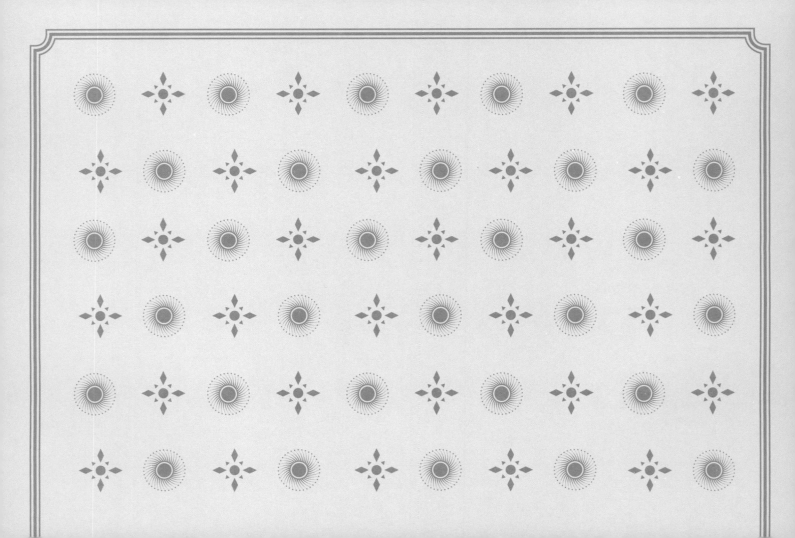

INTENSE & SULTRY

BITTERSWEET SYMPHONY

1 MEASURE GIN

1 MEASURE CAMPARI

½ MEASURE PASSION FRUIT SYRUP

½ MEASURE LEMON JUICE

LEMON, TO GARNISH

Put some ice cubes into a cocktail shaker with all the ingredients and shake to mix.

Strain into an old-fashioned glass over 4–6 ice cubes and garnish with lemon slices.

TANQSTREAM

2 MEASURES TANQUERAY GIN

2 TSP LIME JUICE

3 MEASURES SODA WATER OR TONIC WATER

2 TSP CRÈME DE CASSIS

LIME, TO GARNISH

BLACKCURRANTS OR BLUEBERRIES, TO

GARNISH (OPTIONAL)

Put some cracked ice into a cocktail shaker with the gin and lime juice and shake to mix.

Strain into a highball glass half-filled with cracked ice.

For a dry Tanqstream, add soda water; for a less dry drink, add tonic water.

Stir in the crème de cassis and garnish with lime slices and blackcurrants or blueberries, if you like.

BERRY COLLINS

8 BLUEBERRIES

1–2 DASHES STRAWBERRY SYRUP

4 MEASURES GIN

4 TSP LEMON JUICE

SUGAR SYRUP, TO TASTE

SODA WATER, TO TOP

LEMON, RASPBERRIES & BLUEBERRIES,

TO GARNISH

Muddle the berries and strawberry syrup in the bottom of each glass, then fill each glass with crushed ice.

Add the gin, lemon juice and sugar syrup.

Stir, then top up with the soda water.

Garnish with the berries and a lemon slice.

55

MISSISSIPPI MULE

½ MEASURES GIN

1 TSP CRÈME DE CASSIS

1 TSP LEMON JUICE

Put some ice cubes into a cocktail shaker and pour the gin, crème de cassis and lemon juice over them.

Shake well, strain into a glass and add more ice cubes.

ZED

1 MEASURE GIN

1 MEASURE MANDARINE NAPOLÉON BRANDY

3 MEASURES PINEAPPLE JUICE

1 TSP SUGAR

LEMON, MINT, PINEAPPLE & ORANGE,

TO GARNISH

Put cracked ice into a cocktail shaker and pour the gin, Mandarine Napoléon, pineapple juice and sugar over it.

Shake lightly to mix and pour into a tall glass.

Garnish with half lemon slices, a mint sprig, a pineapple wedge and orange rind strips.

57

FINO HIGHBALL

1 MEASURE GIN

1 MEASURE FINO SHERRY

4 SLICES CLEMENTINE

2 SLICES LEMON

2 TSP PASSION FRUIT SYRUP

2 MEASURES LOW-CALORIE TONIC WATER

LEMON, TO GARNISH

Muddle the fruit in a cocktail shaker, add the gin, sherry and passion fruit syrup.

Fill cocktail shaker with ice cubes and shake, then strain into a glass.

Add the tonic water, fill the glass with crushed ice and garnish with a lemon wedge.

NIGHT OF PASSION

2 MEASURES GIN

1 MEASURE COINTREAU

1 TBSP LEMON JUICE

2 MEASURES PEACH NECTAR

2 TBSP PASSION FRUIT JUICE

Put 3–4 ice cubes into a cocktail shaker with all the ingredients and shake well.

Strain into an old-fashioned glass over another 3–4 ice cubes.

RED KISS

½ MEASURE GIN

1 MEASURE DRY VERMOUTH

½ MEASURE CHERRY BRANDY

COCKTAIL CHERRY & LEMON, TO GARNISH

Put 3 cracked ice cubes into a mixing glass, add the vermouth, gin and cherry brandy and stir well.

Strain into a chilled cocktail glass and garnish with a cocktail cherry and a lemon rind spiral.

FRENCH PINK LADY

2 MEASURES GIN

1 MEASURE TRIPLE SEC

3 TSP LIME JUICE

1 TSP PASTIS

4 RASPBERRIES

LIME, TO GARNISH

Add all the ingredients to a cocktail shaker and muddle.

Fill the shaker with ice and shake, then strain into a glass.

Garnish with a lime wedge.

GIN SLING

6 MEASURES GIN

2 MEASURES CHERRY BRANDY

JUICE OF 1 LEMON

SODA WATER, TO TOP

Add all the ingredients except the soda water to a cocktail shaker and shake with plenty of ice.

Strain into 2 highball glasses filled with ice and top up with soda water.

MAIDEN'S PRAYER

4 MEASURES GIN

4 MEASURES COINTREAU

2 MEASURES ORANGE JUICE

Pour all the ingredients into a cocktail shaker with some ice.

Shake well, then strain into 2 chilled martini glasses.

65

MOON RIVER

1 MEASURE DRY GIN

1 MEASURE APRICOT BRANDY

1 MEASURE COINTREAU

½ MEASURE GALLIANO

½ MEASURE LEMON JUICE

MARASCHINO CHERRIES, TO GARNISH

Put some ice cubes into a cocktail shaker and add the rest of the ingredients.

Shake, then strain, into 2 large chilled martini glasses.

Garnish each with a cherry.

COBBLED SUMMER

4 TSP GIN

6 TSP FINO SHERRY

3 TSP LEMON JUICE

3 TSP RASPBERRY SYRUP

2 TSP SUGAR SYRUP

6 CUBES PINEAPPLE

RASPBERRY, TO GARNISH

Add the pineapple cubes to a cocktail shaker and muddle.

Add the rest of your ingredients and shake.

Strain into a collins glass filled with ice cubes, garnish with a raspberry.

WEST SIDE PINK
FLAMINGO

3 MEASURES GIN OR VODKA

8 MEASURES ROSÉ WINE

8 MEASURES WATERMELON JUICE

1 MEASURE LIME JUICE

2 MEASURES STRAWBERRY PURÉE

1 MEASURE STRAWBERRY SYRUP

2 SPRIGS MINT

MINT, TO GARNISH

Add all the ingredients to a food processor or blender and give it short blitzes to coarsely chop the mint.

Pour into a shallow freezer container and freeze for 24 hours.

Remove from the freezer and stir with a fork to create a granita.

Spoon into 2 wine glasses, each garnished with a mint sprig, and serve with spoon.

69

ORANGE BLOSSOM

2 MEASURES GIN

2 MEASURES PINK GRAPEFRUIT JUICE

2 TSP ORGEAT

2 DASHES ANGOSTURA BITTERS

4 ORANGE SLICES

ORANGE, TO GARNISH

Muddle the orange slices and orgeat in a rocks glass, add the remaining ingredients, fill with crushed ice and churn.

Top with more crushed ice and garnish with orange wedges.

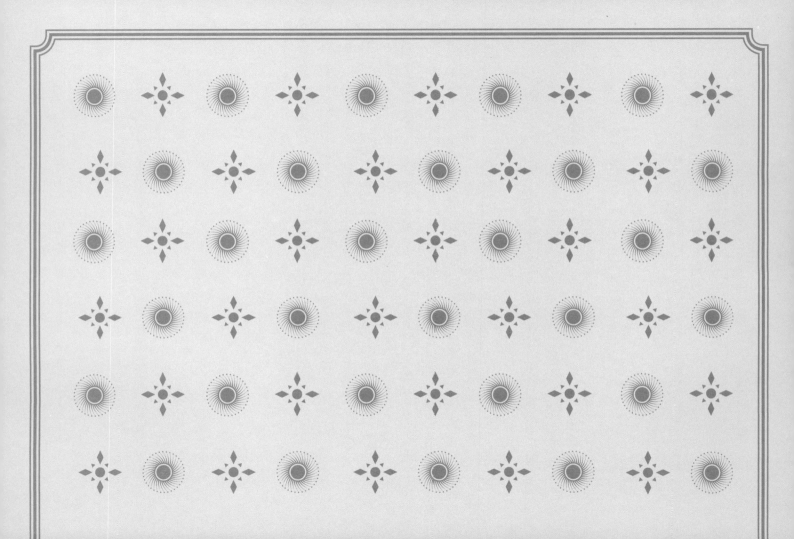

SHARERS & PUNCHES

TWISTED SANGRIA

4 MEASURES GIN

6 MEASURES APPLE JUICE

2 MEASURES LEMON JUICE

2 MEASURES ELDERFLOWER CORDIAL

6 MEASURES WHITE WINE

6 MEASURES SODA WATER

APPLE, LEMON & MINT, TO GARNISH

Fill a jug with ice cubes, add all the ingredients and stir.

Garnish with apple and lemon slices and mint leaves.

GINGER LANGRA

4 MEASURES GINGER & CARDAMOM-

INFUSED GIN (SEE PAGE 115)

4 MEASURES FINO SHERRY

2 MEASURES MANGO JUICE

2 MEASURES LEMON JUICE

2 MEASURES SUGAR SYRUP

200 ML TONIC WATER

LIME, TO GARNISH

Add all the ingredients to a large
jug full of ice cubes and stir.

Garnish with lime wheels.

SYLVESTRE PUNCH

4 MEASURES GIN

1 MEASURE LEMON JUICE

4 MEASURES ORANGE JUICE

4 MEASURES PINK GRAPEFRUIT JUICE

250 ML EARL GREY TEA, CHILLED

1 TBSP MARMALADE

6 MEASURES MINERAL WATER

Add all the ingredients to a food processor to blender and blend until smooth.

Place in a soda syphon and charge with carbon dioxide, following the manufacturer's instructions.

Chill in the refrigerator for at least 1 hour in the soda syphon.

Pour into a large serving bottle to serve.

LANGRA & TONIC

7 MEASURES GIN

4 MEASURES MANGO JUICE

2 MEASURES LEMON JUICE

2 MEASURES SUGAR

200 ML TONIC WATER

LEMON, TO GARNISH

Fill a jug with ice cubes, add all the ingredients and stir.

Garnish with lemon wheels.

PINK LACE PUNCH

4 MEASURES GIN

200 ML ROSÉ WINE

4 MEASURES LYCHEE JUICE

4 MEASURES PINK GRAPEFRUIT JUICE

1 MEASURE LEMON JUICE

1 MEASURE ROSE SYRUP

6 MEASURES SODA WATER

TINNED LYCHEES, LEMON & MARASCHINO

CHERRIES, TO GARNISH

Fill a large jug with ice cubes, add all the ingredients and stir.

Garnish with tinned lychees, lemon slices and maraschino cherries.

HONEYDEW PUNCH

3 MEASURES GIN

1 MEASURE STRAWBERRY LIQUEUR

8 MEASURES HONEYDEW MELON JUICE

2 MEASURES LIME JUICE

2 MEASURES SUGAR SYRUP

1 BUNCH TORN MINT LEAVES

PROSECCO, TO TOP

HONEYDEW MELON, MINT & STRAWBERRIES,

TO GARNISH

Add all the ingredients to a jug or punch bowl filled with cubed ice and stir well.

Garnish with slices of honeydew melon, whole strawberries and sprigs of mint.

EARL'S PUNCH

4 MEASURES GIN

6 MEASURES EARL GREY TEA, CHILLED

6 MEASURES PINK GRAPEFRUIT JUICE

6 MEASURES SODA WATER

1 MEASURE SUGAR SYRUP

PINK GRAPEFRUIT SLICES & BLACK

CHERRIES, TO GARNISH

Fill a jug with ice cubes, add all the remaining ingredients and stir.

Garnish with pink grapefruit slices and black cherries.

ON THE LAWN

2 MEASURES GIN

2 MEASURES PIMM'S NO. 1 CUP

LEMONADE & GINGER ALE, TO TOP

STRAWBERRIES

ORANGES

Fill 2 highball glasses with ice and fresh fruit such as strawberries and peeled orange segments.

Add the Pimm's No. 1 Cup and gin to each one and top up with lemonade and ginger ale.

ENGLISH GARDEN FIZZ

500 ML LONDON DRY GIN

250 ML TRIPLE SEC

250 ML LEMON JUICE

250 ML SUGAR SYRUP

250 ML APPLE JUICE

500 ML GREEN TEA, CHILLED

500 ML SODA WATER

1 BUNCH MINT LEAVES

CUCUMBER, TO GARNISH

85

Add the gin and 1 bunch mint leaves to a large punch bowl and leave to infuse for 1 hour.

Remove the mint, add the rest of the ingredients and some ice cubes to the punch bowl.

Stir and garnish with cucumber slices.

GARDEN COOLER

700 ML LONDON DRY GIN

500 ML LEMON JUICE

250 ML SUGAR SYRUP

250 ML ELDERFLOWER CORDIAL

500 ML GREEN TEA, CHILLED

500 ML MINT TEA, CHILLED

500 ML APPLE JUICE

500 ML SODA WATER

PEACH, TO GARNISH

Add all the ingredients and a generous amount of ice cubes to a punch bowl and stir.

Garnish with peach slices.

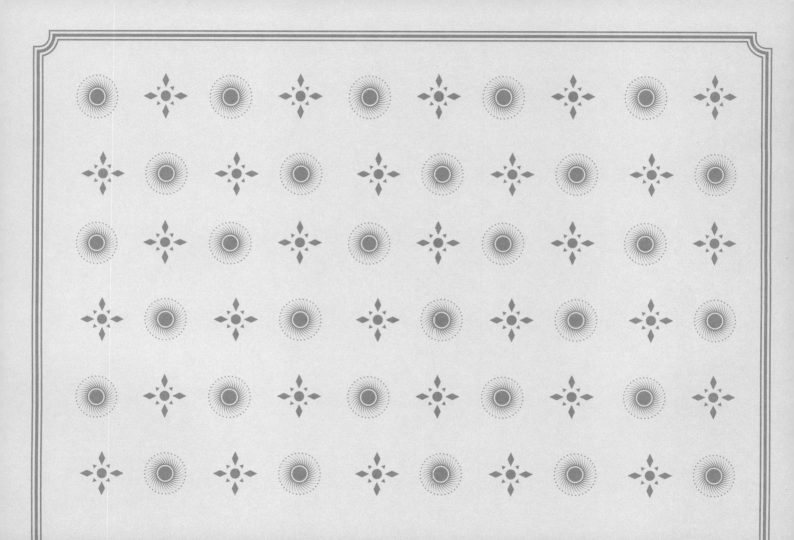

TOM COLLINS

2 MEASURES GIN

1 MEASURE LEMON JUICE

1 MEASURE SUGAR SYRUP

4 MEASURES SODA WATER

LEMON & BLACK CHERRY, TO GARNISH

Put all the ingredients except the soda water into cocktail shaker and fill with ice cubes.

Shake then strain into a glass full of ice cubes and top up with the soda water.

Garnish with a lemon wedge and a black cherry.

SINGAPORE SLING

2 MEASURES GIN

1 MEASURE CHERRY BRANDY

½ MEASURE COINTREAU

½ MEASURE BÉNÉDICTINE

1 MEASURE GRENADINE

1 MEASURE LIME JUICE

10 MEASURES PINEAPPLE JUICE

1–2 DASHES ANGOSTURA BITTERS

PINEAPPLE & MARASCHINO CHERRIES,

TO GARNISH

Half-fill a cocktail shaker with ice cubes, add the remaining ingredients and shake until a frost forms on the outside of the shaker.

Strain into 2 highball glasses and garnish each one with a pineapple wedge and a maraschino cherry.

GIMLET

2 ½ MEASURES GIN

½ MEASURE LIME CORDIAL

½ MEASURE LIME JUICE

LIME, TO GARNISH

Add all the ingredients to your cocktail shaker, shake and strain into a chilled cocktail glass.

Garnish with a lime rind spiral.

NEGRONI

1 MEASURE GIN

1 MEASURE SWEET VERMOUTH

1 MEASURE CAMPARI

ORANGE, TO GARNISH

Fill a glass with ice cubes, add all the ingredients and stir.

Garnish with an orange wedge.

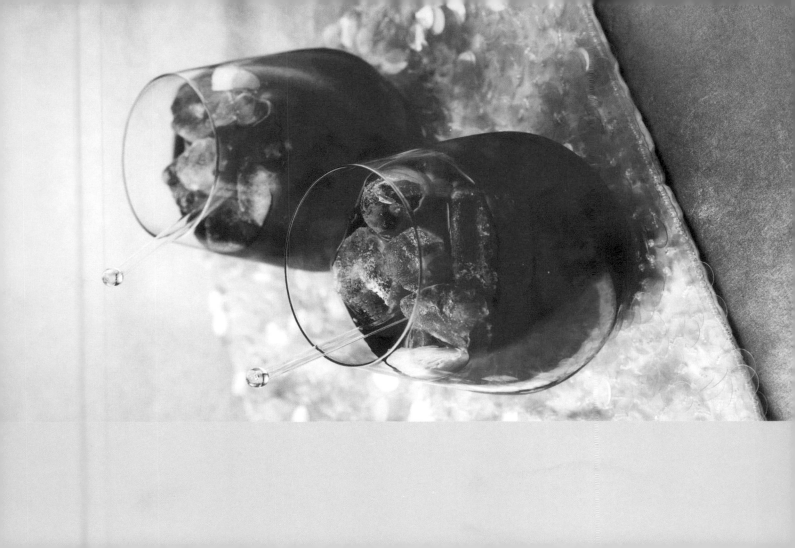

MONKEY GLAND

1 MEASURE ORANGE JUICE

2 MEASURES GIN

3 DASHES PERNOD

3 DASHES GRENADINE

Put 3–4 ice cubes into a cocktail shaker with all the ingredients.

Shake well, then strain into a chilled cocktail glass.

PINK GIN

2 MEASURES GIN

5 DASHES ANGOSTURA BITTERS

STILL WATER, TO TOP

Add all ingredients to an old
fashioned glass filled with cubed ice
and stir briefly before serving.

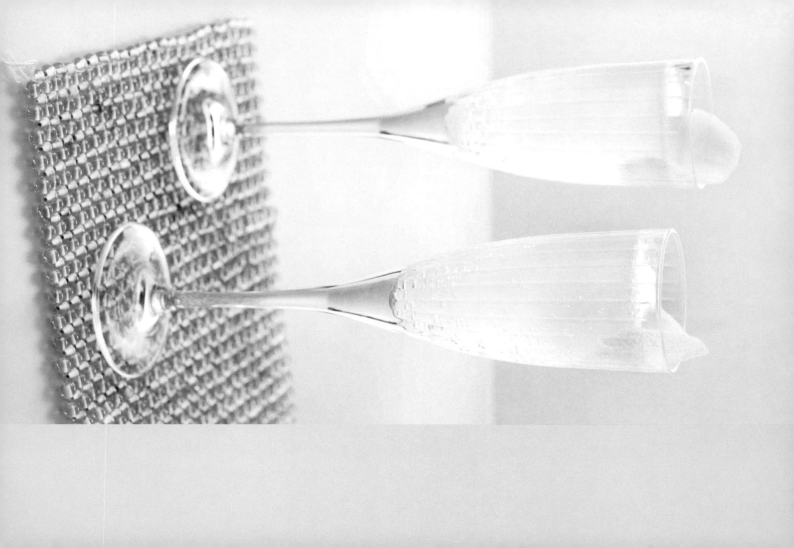

FRENCH 75

1 MEASURE GIN

3 TSP LEMON JUICE

3 TSP SUGAR SYRUP

4 MEASURES CHAMPAGNE, TO TOP

LEMON, TO GARNISH

Add all the ingredients, except the Champagne, to a cocktail shaker and shake.

Strain into a flute glass and top up with chilled Champagne.

Garnish with a lemon twist.

SOUTHSIDE ROYALE

1 ½ MEASURES GIN

¾ MEASURE LIME JUICE

¾ MEASURE SUGAR SYRUP

6 MINT LEAVES

PROSECCO, TO TOP

MINT, TO GARNISH

Add all the ingredients to your cocktail shaker, shake vigorously and double strain into a chilled cocktail glass.

Top with Prosecco and garnish with a mint leaf.

AVIATION

2 MEASURES GIN

½ MEASURE MARASCHINO LIQUEUR

½ MEASURE LEMON JUICE

COCKTAIL CHERRY, TO GARNISH

Put some ice cubes into a cocktail shaker with the gin, maraschino liqueur and lemon juice.

Shake well and double strain into a chilled martini glass.

Garnish with a cocktail cherry on a cocktail stick.

LONG ISLAND ICED TEA

1 MEASURE GIN

1 MEASURE VODKA

1 MEASURE WHITE RUM

1 MEASURE TEQUILA

1 MEASURE COINTREAU

1 MEASURE LEMON JUICE

COLA, TO TOP

LEMON, TO GARNISH

Add all the ingredients, except the cola, in a cocktail shaker with some ice cubes and shake to mix.

Strain into 2 highball glasses filled with ice cubes and top up with cola.

Garnish with lemon slices.

FLORADORA

2 MEASURES GIN

½ TSP GRENADINE

JUICE OF ½ LIME

½ TSP SUGAR SYRUP

DRY GINGER ALE, TO TOP

LIME, TO GARNISH

Put 4–5 ice cubes into a cocktail shaker, add the remaining ingredients and shake until a frost forms.

Pour without straining into a hurricane glass, top up with ginger ale and garnish with a lime rind twist.

GIN FIZZ

2 MEASURES PLYMOUTH GIN

1 MEASURE LEMON JUICE

2–3 DASHES SUGAR SYRUP

¼ EGG WHITE, BEATEN

SODA WATER, TO TOP

LEMON SLICES & ROSEMARY, TO GARNISH

Put some ice cubes into a cocktail shaker with the gin, lemon juice, sugar syrup and egg white.

Shake to mix and strain into a highball glass.

Top up with soda water and garnish with lemon slices and a rosemary sprig.

105

CLASSIC MARTINI

6 MEASURES GIN

1 MEASURE DRY VERMOUTH

STUFFED GREEN OLIVES, TO GARNISH

Put 10–12 ice cubes into a mixing glass.

Pour over the vermouth and gin and stir (never shake) vigorously and evenly without splashing.

Strain into 2 chilled martini glasses, garnish each with a green olive.

107

CLOVER CLUB

2 MEASURES GIN

¾ MEASURE LEMON JUICE

¾ MEASURE SUGAR SYRUP

5 RASPBERRIES

½ MEASURE EGG WHITE

RASPBERRIES, TO GARNISH

Add all the ingredients to your cocktail shaker and dry shake without ice for 10 seconds.

Take the shaker apart, add cubed ice and shake vigorously.

Strain into a cocktail glass and garnish with raspberries.

VESPER MARTINI

2 ½ MEASURES GIN

1 MEASURE VODKA

½ MEASURE LILLET BLANC WINE

LEMON, TO GARNISH

Add all the ingredients into the bottom of your cocktail shaker, and fill the top half of it with ice.

Shake vigorously and double strain into a chilled martini glass.

Garnish with a lemon twist.

PIMM'S COCKTAIL

2 MEASURES PIMM'S NO. 1 CUP

2 MEASURES GIN

4 MEASURES LEMONADE

4 MEASURES GINGER ALE

CUCUMBER, BLUEBERRIES & ORANGE,

TO GARNISH

Add all the ingredients evenly between 2 highball glasses filled with ice cubes.

Garnish with cucumber strips, orange slices and blueberries.

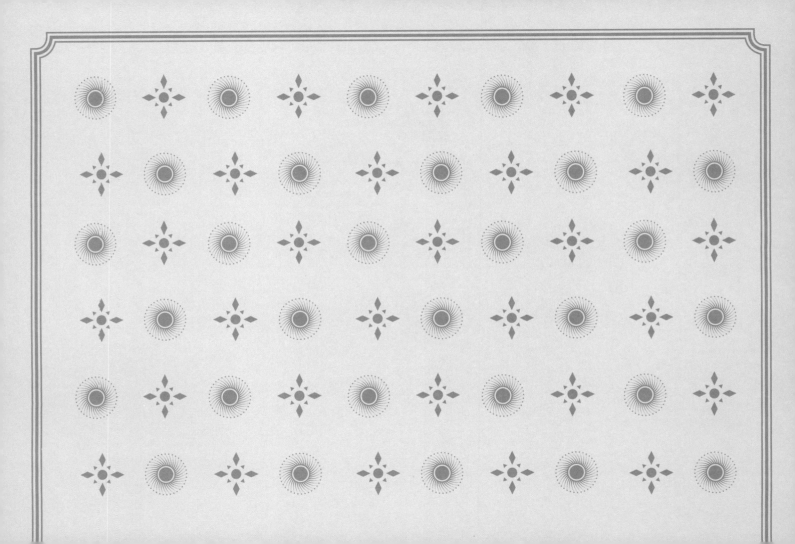

TIPS & TECHNIQUES FOR CRAFTING THE PERFECT COCKTAIL

WHAT MAKES A GOOD COCKTAIL?

Good cocktails, like good food, are based around quality ingredients. As with cooking, using fresh and homemade ingredients can often make the huge difference between a good drink and an outstanding drink. All of this can be found in department stores, online or in kitchen shops.

COCKTAIL INGREDIENTS

ICE   This is a key part of cocktails and you'll need lots of it. Purchase it from your supermarket or freeze big tubs of water, then crack this up to use in your drinks. If you're hosting a big party and want to serve some punches, which will need lots of ice, it may be worthwhile finding if you have a local ice supplier that supplies catering companies, as this can be much more cost effective.

CITRUS JUICE   It's important to use fresh citrus juice in your drinks; bottled versions taste awful and will not produce good drinks. Store your fruit out of the refrigerator at room temperature. Look for a soft-skinned fruit for juicing, which you can do with a

juicer or citrus press. You can keep fresh
citrus juice for a couple of days in the
refrigerator, sealed to prevent oxidation.

SUGAR SYRUP You can buy sugar syrup or
you can make your own. The most basic form
of sugar syrup is made by mixing caster sugar
and hot water together, and stirring until the
sugar has dissolved. The key when preparing
sugar syrups is to use a 1:1 ratio of sugar to
liquid. White sugar acts as a flavour enhancer,
while dark sugars have unique, more toffee
flavours and work well with dark spirits.

BASIC SUGAR SYRUP RECIPE
(Makes 1 litre (1¾ pints) of sugar syrup)
Dissolve 1 kg (2 lb) caster sugar in 1 litre
(1¾ pints) of hot water.
Allow to cool.
Sugar syrup will keep in a sterilized bottle
stored in the refrigerator for up to 2 weeks.

CUCUMBER-INFUSED GIN
Add ½ medium cucumber to 500 ml (17 fl oz)
gin, white rum or vodka and leave to infuse
for 24 hours.

GINGER & CARDAMOM-INFUSED GIN
Add 100 g (3½ oz) fresh root ginger, peeled
and sliced, and 1 teaspoon green cardamom
pods to 500 ml (17 fl oz) and leave to infuse for
2 days.

CHOOSING GLASSWARE

There are many different cocktails, but they all fall into one of three categories: long, short or shot. Long drinks generally have more mixer than alcohol, often served with ice and a straw. The terms 'straight up' and 'on the rocks' are synonymous with the short drink, which tends to be more about the spirit, often combined with a single mixer at most. Finally, there is the shot which is made up mainly from spirits and liqueurs, designed to give a quick hit of alcohol. Glasses are tailored to the type of drinks they will contain.

CHAMPAGNE FLUTE Used for Champagne or Champagne cocktails, the narrow mouth of the flute helps the drink to stay fizzy.

CHAMPAGNE SAUCER A classic glass, but not very practical for serving Champagne as the drink quickly loses its fizz.

MARGARITA OR COUPETTE GLASS When used for a Margarita, the rim is dipped in salt. Also used for daiquiris and other fruit-based cocktails.

HIGHBALL GLASS Suitable for any long cocktail, such as a Long Island Iced Tea.

COLLINS GLASS This is similar to a highball glass but is slightly narrower.

WINE GLASS Sangria is often served in one, but they are not usually used for cocktails.

OLD-FASHIONED GLASS Also known as a rocks glass, this is great for any drink that's served on the rocks or straight up.

SHOT GLASS Often found in two sizes — for a single or double measure. They are ideal for a single mouthful.

BALLOON GLASS Often used for fine spirits. The glass can be warmed to encourage the release of the drink's aroma.

HURRICANE GLASS Mostly found in beach bars, used for creamy, rum-based drinks.

BOSTON GLASS Often used by bartenders for mixing cocktails, good for fruity drinks.

TODDY GLASS A toddy glass is generally used for a hot drink, such as Irish Coffee.

SLING GLASS This has a very short stemmed base and is most famously used for a Singapore Sling.

MARTINI GLASS Also known as a cocktail glass, its thin neck design makes sure your hand can't warm the glass, or the cocktail.

USEFUL EQUIPMENT

Some pieces of equipment, such as shakers and the correct glasses, are vital for any cocktail party, while others, like ice buckets, can be obtained at a later date if needed. Below is a wishlist for anyone who wants to make cocktails on a regular basis.

SHAKER The Boston shaker is the most simple option, but it needs to be used in conjunction with a hawthorne strainer. Alternatively you could choose a shaker with a built-in strainer.

MEASURE OR JIGGER Single and double measures are available and are essential when you are mixing ingredients so that the proportions are always the same. One measure is 25 ml or 1 fl oz.

MIXING GLASS A mixing glass is used for those drinks that require only a gentle stirring before they are poured or strained.

HAWTHORNE STRAINER This type of strainer is often used in conjunction with a Boston shaker, but a simple tea strainer will also work well.

BAR SPOON Similar to a teaspoon but with a long handle, a bar spoon is used for stirring, layering and muddling drinks.

MUDDLING STICK Similar to a pestle, which will work just as well, a muddling stick, or muddler, is used to crush fruit or herbs in a glass or shaker for drinks like the Mojito.

BOTTLE OPENER Choose a bottle opener with two attachments, one for metal-topped bottles and a corkscrew for wine bottles.

POURERS A pourer is inserted into the top of a spirit bottle to enable the spirit to flow in a controlled manner.

FOOD PROCESSOR A food processor or blender is useful for making frozen cocktails and smoothies.

EQUIPMENT FOR GARNISHING Many drinks are garnished with fruit on cocktail sticks and these are available in wood, plastic or glass. Exotic drinks may be prettified with a paper umbrella and several long drinks are served with straws or swizzle sticks.

TECHNIQUES

With just a few basic techniques, your bartending skills will be complete. Follow the instructions to hone your craft.

BLENDING Frozen cocktails and smoothies are blended with ice in a blender until they are of a smooth consistency. Be careful not to add too much ice as this will dilute the cocktail. It's best to add a little at a time.

SHAKING The best-known cocktail technique and probably the most common. Used to mix ingredients thoroughly and quickly, and to chill the drink before serving.
1 Half-fill a cocktail shaker with ice cubes, or cracked or crushed ice.
2 If the recipe calls for a chilled glass add a few ice cubes and some cold water to the glass, swirl it around and discard.
3 Add the ingredients to the shaker and shake until a frost forms on the outside.
4 Strain the cocktail into the glass and serve.

MUDDLING A technique used to bring out the flavours of herbs and fruit using a blunt tool called a muddler.
1 Add chosen herb(s) to a highball glass. Add some sugar syrup and some lime wedges.
2 Hold the glass firmly and use a muddler or pestle to twist and press down.

3 Continue for 30 seconds, top up with crushed ice and add remaining ingredients.

DOUBLE-STRAINING To prevent all traces of puréed fruit and ice fragments from entering the glass, use a shaker with a built-in strainer in conjunction with a hawthorne strainer. A fine strainer also works well.

LAYERING Some spirits can be served layered on top of each other, causing 'lighter' spirits to float on top of your cocktail.
1 Pour the first ingredient into a glass, taking care that it does not touch the sides.
2 Position a bar spoon in the centre of the glass, rounded part down and facing you. Rest the spoon against the side of the glass as your pour the second ingredient down the spoon. It should float on top of the first liquid.
3 Repeat with the third ingredient, then carefully remove the spoon.

STIRRING Used when the ingredients need to be mixed and chilled, but also maintain their clarity. This ensures there are no ice fragments or air bubbles throughout the drink. Some cocktails require the ingredients to be prepared in a mixing glass, then strained into the serving glass.
1 Add ingredients to a glass, in recipe order.
2 Use a bar spoon to stir the drink, lightly or vigorously, as described in the recipe.
3 Finish the drink with any decoration and serve.

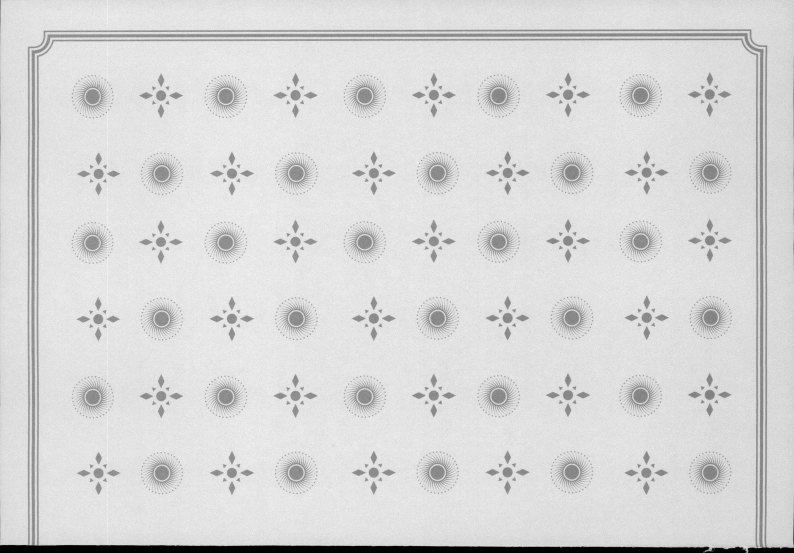

INDEX

PICTURE CREDITS

Octopus Publishing Group Jonathan Kennedy 13, 16, 29, 34, 39, 43, 46, 58, 63, 70, 74, 79, 82, 87, 91, 95, 98; Stephen Conroy 21, 54, 67, 103, 106, 111.